T0284435

Five-Paragraph Essay
on the Body-Mind Problem

Wesleyan Poetry

Five-Paragraph Essay on the Body-Mind Problem

Rachel Trousdale

Wesleyan University Press
Middletown, Connecticut

Wesleyan University Press
Middletown, CT 06459
www.wesleyan.edu/wespress

© 2025 Rachel Trousdale
All rights reserved
Printed in Canada
Designed and composed in Cochin and Source Sans types
by Chris Crochetière of BW&A Books, Inc.
Art credit: William Morris, Wallpaper Blackberry Pattern,
Art Heritage / Alamy Stock Photo

Library of Congress Cataloging-in-Publication Data
available at https://catalog.loc.gov/
paper   ISBN 978-0-8195-0185-1
ebook   ISBN 978-0-8195-0186-8

5 4 3 2 1

for Nick

Contents

I. Introduction

Five-Paragraph Essay on the Body-Mind Problem

I love you because you are a unique snowflake. The extent to which a snowflake can be unique is subject to debate. Humans share 25 percent of their DNA with bananas. Given two humans, fallen onto the coat sleeve of a Brobdingnag, would it be possible to tell us apart? To tell us from bananas? The yellow bananas found in American supermarkets are genetically interchangeable.

You are pale and interesting. Blood vessels can be constricted by infecting the subject with the tuberculosis bacillus; dehydration; blood loss; or the ingestion of large quantities of vinegar. Pallor can be applied in the form of clown white, greasepaint, or foundation makeup. Tuberculosis patients with a hectic flush were considered attractive circa 1893; given the bacillus's long incubation period, it is hard to ascertain resultant infection rates.

But the epidemiology of love can be tracked through the progress of syphilis. Joints become inflamed, and the patient walks with a characteristic stifflegged gait. Spirochetes invade the brain, and he suffers increasing dementia. Cerebral syphilitic infection can be differentiated from the euphoria of love by an examination of the spinal fluid.

Please do not bathe or change your clothes until further notice; any alteration in your location, pose, mood, etc., will be breach of contract and grounds for legal action. To facilitate your stasis I will provide you with a regular supply of bananas. Should prolonged inactivity produce stiffness, a diagnosis of syphilis should not be ruled out, and mercury treatments should be considered. Mercury is named after the Roman messenger of the gods, perhaps for the speed at which the liquid metal moves. Treatments can be fatal, but are preferred to the disease; patients may, however, regret their lost noses.

Sans nose, sans eyes, sans teeth, sans everything, there will nonetheless be a systematic endorphin release when I see you; there may also be a significant rise in adrenaline from sexual attraction, which when examined through a stethoscope is indistinguishable from rage. How come I can never tell what you are thinking?

The Reef

for Nick

Just because it's made doesn't mean it's anything
but natural. A thin line skirting the shore, no matter
how long, it appears tiny in the extent of
the ocean it inhabits, the water that is the only thing
that makes it invisible from the moon. Minute and
enormous, to build one would be an impossible
ambition, and yet now and then people, who have destroyed
so many, try in restitution to drop in old subway cars,
holed ship carcasses, their various failed transports,
guilt offerings to the ocean, which does not ask for them,
seeded with first inhabitants — corals who never
imagined themselves a city or wall but produce their cells
and turn the sea salts slowly into limestone.
Piece by piece it is unconsciously assembled:
if the currents are neither too hot nor too cold,
and if those on shore refrain from dumping oil and ashes
too lavishly into the streams, if the ocean bed
is neither too roughly scrubbed by storms nor too unstirred,
slowly the thing will accrete; just as a few minutes
turn into a lifetime, a few infinitesimal manylegged
brief shy creatures become a reef. Building on each other,
each kind makes its own fanciful, bizarre formations:
orange antlers; fluted pipe organs; pink hearts; inhabited
by eels, which shock, and octopi, which change
color and shape at whim, and can compress themselves
into a crevice or expand like a canopy, and die
in the care of their young; each on its own
a study, but each a part, if luck and the currents
hold, of mile upon mile of variegated
whole. The fish, who are not concerned with the flick of rainbow
white at the surface, pass like particulate smoke;
the little striped clownfish burrows into his friendly
poisonous anemone. Somewhere in the crowd
is every color, but silver and blue predominate,

4

lit with yellow, spiked with vermilion. Here
is God's plenty, if we believed in God. Instead
we worry that somewhere must be a barracuda,
a reef shark, a magnificent giant stingray; fate
lurks—but that is only to say that individuals
are mortal, which we knew. The reef is time made visible,
its profusion and proliferation, its vivacity,
its wealth instantaneous and enduring. To say
that it is like something would be presumptuous,
but perhaps, in a limited way, a marriage is
like it—something that began with a few small motions
and has turned, by grace of time, into—not an edifice—
a beautiful sprawl, a forest, a live extent.
For this, maybe, we fly south, we don our masks
and fins and dive into an element not our own:
to see something like, or more than like, the thing we have made.

Optics Lab

This is not a sestina, it's a hologram.
When I was eight, or about eight, my father
took me to the darkened optics lab
in the science tower basement, and showed me
a single floating dot, a disappointing dot
he helped six students make with a laser.

That's how you make sestinas—with a laser.
I mean that's how you make holograms.
You point two or six or ninety-two beams at an object
and bounce light off it, and show it to my father.
He detects an image in the waves, and tells me
it is formed by interference; in the lab

he described his work in other labs
amplifying light by stimulated emission of radiation—
honestly: he helped invent the laser: he tells me;
but how does this dot become a sticker with a prancing silver unicorn?
How do I describe my father?
Who is ninety-two today, a floating candle flame

on a cake; who is singular;
who explained about the two-slit experiment
when I was eight. He is still himself,
mostly. While his lab was fine-tuning that first laser,
he might have guessed about holograms,
but "I wouldn't have believed you if you'd told me"

about supermarket scanners, CDs, cat toys. Time
tells. Time passes, and that disappointing dot
is rainbow, landscape, animal. To make a hologram
you record perspectives on a light field
and illuminate the tracks left by your laser
until in parallax you create my father.

I visited today and said to my father,
"I'm writing a sestina. Explain light for me."
We looked at each other.
His explanation dwindled to a dot.
He gestured at the moving, silent world.
"Rachel, I can't." He is a hologram,

an image, an incomplete experiment,
a pattern that can almost write the whole.

Variations on a Theme by Oscar Wilde

Pleasure is the only thing one should live for. Nothing ages like happiness.
—Wilde, *Miscellanies*

At lunch, I quote the White Queen: *Jam to-morrow,*
and jam yesterday—but never jam to-day. My daughter laughs:
"Is that a poem?" She, almost three, how does she know?
She is all jam, tiger-striped in apricot; she hears the rhythm, the fall
of artifice. She delights to eat, to recognize, to know. Drapes
herself across my belly to nurse, at her age! beneath a yellow blanket.
    Consumes
everything she cares for: the thin flow of milk;
her brother's embrace; a whole box of fig newtons, stealthily,
braced against the guest room door to prevent intrusions. "Mommy,
    are you happy?"
then, "But are you sad that Uncle Chris is gone?" She disapproves:
"You are a lot of things. But I'm just Ellie." Is that a poem?
    What does she know
about happiness? Long before her appetite, my grandfather
found his wife's father lying on the guest room bed, shaven, blue suit,
    a long kitchen knife
harmless across his chest. "I'm going to kill myself," he said. But
my grandfather said, "Why don't you wait until after lunch?"

Dreams from the Eastern State Pen, 1829

for Charles Williams, two years' solitary confinement with labor

He is eighteen and he has been eighteen.
He dreams his hands the color of the walls.

He's fed. A door is opened twice a day
onto a roofless room. He sees the sky,

the grass that grows inside that second room,
the rain if it is raining, or the snow.

His hands aren't yet the color of the walls.
There is a book. Its words are strange. It's black.

He dreams he'd heard of it when he could hear.
It's old. He is to read it every day.

He dreams the angels' trumpets all are stopped.
The book stays sealed upon the angel's hands.

The angel is the color of the walls.
The book is still the color of his hands.

The seals are red as nothing. Nothing red
was ever in this room.

He has a bench and hammers to make shoes.
He dreams he hears the nails protest aloud

when he surrounds them with the leather sole.
The leather hurts them, it is rough as rock.

He cannot make them quiet. So he takes
the nails next time he gains the other room

And leaves them in the grass. They are still there
the next dream and the next. After the rain

they blush from black to orange-red in shame
because they cannot hide against the walls.

II. First Body Paragraph

Love Poem with Dereliction of Duty

It's true—I like you more than I like
the Marquis de Sade; God that
mid-April afternoon in 1995,
when I said, let's take a walk
and you said sure and we circled
the New Haven Green saying
who the hell knows what
because if we had seen
all this falling in love stuff coming, we
would have paid more attention;
I just know it took two hours,
past the churches and the porn shop
and over to the cemetery with all
those skull-topped slabs leaning
memorially against the brownstone wall;
round and round we went like marbles
dodging the traps in a game
of labyrinth; and finally back
to campus through that big stone gate
which we entered just as the prof
of the philosophy class I was skipping
came out and I said oh the pain
the pain I can't take it any more
and doubled up laughing

Your Airplane

he says and hands me
all that terrible solid wind through which
we have risen and through which
I now if I twitch too hard can make us fall;
"Lower" he says and I press my hands forward
to a change in the noise, a buck, a hum
and for the first time I have
no faith in my pilot,
no reassurance against the leaps of the air;
"Steeper" he says and the air is
fighting the wings, he and I
are in the air's hands
and for all my love
of the sequence of cause and effect,
for all my hope that we can steer
through hurricanes,
for all my ambition and
desire for exaltation
this leap is too much leap and I
cannot take this one, I
fail this test, I say, enough,
your airplane

Invisible Mice

in his apartment. They're quick. I can't get a good look,
but they remind me of the little moles
the cat used to bring in: soft, but with teeth.
He says, There are no droppings. There's no mice.
But I can see them every night I'm there.
He says, It's just your eyes. You know you do
see spots. But that's before my migraines.
I have no migraine now. Last night they were
darting along the mopboards like the fish
in an aquarium, like that huge tank
in Boston, where the further down you go
past shoals of silver and reflected feet,
the bigger and the stranger come the sharks.

Furnishing

We took the sofa and stood it on its right arm against the window. We took the new Japanese kitchen knife and made horizontal slots in the sofa. The sofa cushions bled little yellow crumbles onto the floor, so we swept them up and put them in the sugar bowl. Along the shelves we hung the clothes hangers, and from them we draped electrical cords we had severed from the bodies of machines. The cat ran up and down the ramps of the shelves and made the cords swing. The lamps we grouped in the bedroom, five in a circle in the center of the mattress in the center of the room.

Finally I sat in the bathtub in my winter coat and you came in and turned the shower on cold. "Welcome home," you said. "Welcome home," I said. So we left.

Self-Portrait as Noble Pen Shell

Patience. Neptune grass grows at the rate
of three cm per year. Blooms. Shelters
moray eels; seahorses; the larvae
of *pinna nobilis*, which, rooted,
mature, achieve a height above four feet.
Even the mixed fescue out your window
beneath the unexpected cover of
mid-April snow is growing, now, somehow,
if not fresh shoots then roots, gathering strength.
Is that something you lack? All right; you lack it.
You lack also an aragonite shell
to fend off predators; you fail, repeatedly,
to feed yourself on light. If only time
were passing at the rate of one second
per second. If you only slept,
occasionally, all night. If only
you'd scooped, this morning, paired handfuls of snow,
and found six intact violets, waiting—
tomorrow, next day at the latest—for
the bees.

I Swear This Is Not Intended as a Back-Handed Compliment

Being with you is as good
as being alone: think
what that means—the impossible
luxury of silence, my own warmth,
the ease of nakedness. Nothing
to adapt to; no demand of response;
nothing but the law of gravity
to contradict me—God, sometimes
I miss it, the way the world
imposed nothing on me
when I was alone in my first apartment
with its terrible brown ceiling
and ridiculous white floors.
And being with you is as good.

Lost in the Woods

As I wander into you, I drop, every fourth step,
a white pebble, round and clean
as a skull, in the closing avenue of trees.
There's something ahead: a light? a fire?
the phosphorescent breathing of the swamp?
There's bread in my pocket. I'll find out.
But the woods are full of warblers, little
brown flickering things.
Lacking their own teeth, they require
something definitive with which to grind
their food. They flick, they stoop.
Slowly the path behind me disappears.

Love Poem with Boojum

Traversing tramontane gullies; evading the swoops of pteradactloid unfamiliar not-ospreys; frostbitten, wind-chapped, heavy-hearted; encumbered with sheepskins, canvas, bundles of firing; footsore, irate; writing each night in a warped leather journal the longitude and the day's losses—Bearer slipped into crevasse. Donkey mauled by bear.—but persevering, ever on the impossible hunt; whittled to sinew, wind-browned, hair bleached by the driven sand, eyes drawn into an eternal squint; dried, sharpened; barely warmed by the barley soup, the bitter thin tea, the native dung-fires; skirting the base of the glacier looming beautifully, uncrossably above, lending always a tang of perfect mummification to the air; until, after descending a particularly precipitous escarpment, frangible scree ricocheting under the mukluks, a view into a deep green valley, six distant moss-roofed huts sending just-detectable sweet cedar smoke above their blooming—can it be spring?—cherry trees—and barely visible, some human figure, in a blue tunic, carrying, maybe, a bucket, maybe water from a spring, when I turn and find—

Love Poem with Naratriptan

Like everyone I love, you are
not infallible. I must not approach you
too early, too late; you require
attentive timing. But when I
catch you right, you raise the sky
to its proper height. My darling,
no one could possibly take away
all the nausea of living, forestall
my body's accusations
of neglect—but you
mitigate the indignity of
unnecessary dissolutions.
I promise to take care, to eat enough,
to turn off the light half an hour early,
if you'll catch me when despite
my best intentions I fail.

Units of Measure

Everyone is wrong about eternity. It ebbs
and flows. Think about the distance
between the earth and the sun; then scale that
to Jupiter; to Pluto; well—that is as the distance
between the belly of a snake and the crumbling
brown dirt it slides upon in the face of the distance
between us and even Proxima Centauri. Think
about the time that has passed since we first
walked upright; since scale first
lapped scale—those heavy-skulled reptiles,
the earliest fish. Even the air
was of another substance then. All our many seas
were then one sea. Even that was only
the time it takes to pause at the stop sign
on an abandoned midnight road on a long drive
(south all night through the pine woods, past the farms,
another hour, another four hours before
you can stop to sleep) next to the time since our
hot liquid earth first started cooling.
How long have I loved you? How long
have we loved these children? How
long will anyone know these words? As long
as men can breathe or eyes can see we can keep
trying, keep pushing, keep making
our many mistakes. If I keep driving
one more hour (as the January night extends
toward that distant little January dawn) I think
you can get us home.

III. Second Body Paragraph

Bubble

            is the baby's
first clear word. He is learning
to generalize: lamp globes, flowers,
ferns, sea foam, anything fragile
and desirable and bright. With his word
he points out the moon
as we walk to the vigil. Bubble!
We are on our way to mourn
more Black men murdered. One's name
meant Friend of Man. It is past
bedtime, but the baby trots
as though he could walk forever, stay awake
until justice is brought in, after dinner,
like a cake. There is singing;
we have lit candles. Someone invisible speaks
about hope. Bubble! The baby
reaches for the flame.

Entropy

is like a baby, or a brood of termites;
everything's edible, and nothing's enough.
Here, I say, is a nice clean kitchen for you to play with.
But no: he has to have the bathroom too,
and the whole dining room table,
and even the bookshelves, who were supposed to be working;
he wants to lick the salt of your hands off
everything they've touched, wants
to leave his tooth marks in rings on the sideboard,
wants to chew on the roots of trees and the house's foundations,
and regardless of when you'll be ready, when he's really hungry,
never mind that you're right in the middle of
scribbling something down or kneading the bread dough,
when he's done tasting and testing and spitting things out,
you know he'll be urgently, irrefusably turning
his head to your breast.

Avalanche Conditions

The everlasting universe of things
flows through the mind: pairing the tiny socks;
packed lunch, except on Tuesdays; show and tell;
and dishes. Snow by snow
the mountain seems to grow, even to gentle
its outcroppings and cliffs, softened to smooth
white pillows.
                        All those drifts
are nothing to the granite underneath—
which must be there—unless it's caves of dragons?—
no—alpine tunnels, full of heavy trucks
carrying sustenance between the valleys.
Mountains sustain utility—
and so the drifts grow deeper, carved to sharp
new edges by the winds.
                        One note
sung by a tiny alpinist, and down
roll three small flakes; one shiver; then five hundred thousand tons
of ice shards, sheer implacable dense mass.

For a Child Drowned Off Lesbos

Cupid, come: your image lies breathing softly
on my breast. But infants are all your image;
tender, milky, meltingly fat, they aim your
    merciless arrow,

loose it. Final cause of desire, you make us
makers. Letters tracing a lovely outline,
beauty's faint reflection, in paint or marble—
    never Apollo!—

you, the only origin, make our actions
matter, form, material, make our yearnings
shaped, substantial, plentiful. Not the
    overdetermined

sperm and egg, that binary isolation;
you are friction, motherhood, madness, softness.
Gently my baby awakens, snuffles,
    burrows against me.

How then can you watch as his image nestles
face down on cold sand? Cupid, those narrow
shoulders slid so gracefully to the tide line,
    shaped for their exit

from a clenching womb. He has all your features,
rounded limbs, implacable softness. Only
no more breath. Please; speak to your mother; she knows
    waves and the art of

rising from them. Speak to us. Drive us with your
endless stinging arsenal. Make his heartbeat
all our rapture, all our essential; drowning,
    see that he drowns us.

Our Colt

Let's not pretend it isn't difficult
for everyone. Look: if you make the rent
and eat right now, you'd better be content.
But try explaining to our yearling colt
with April susurrating in his blood
that he must wait; defer to thundercloud; ·
ware lightning. Watch him skittershy and jolt
against the stable door. Rainwater plays
in deltas down the windows. Crash. The ways
of safety are not his. I'd be a dolt
to hold him if I had a choice. Grown men
are cautious, but not him. Thunder again;
oh God—one rumble more and he will bolt.

Syllabus

Goldenrod, brambles. The yellow and black
spider zipping shut its web. We pass:
birches, maples, oaks. What have we taught
our son this sunny summer? Not to mind
the narrow bloody trace left on your shin
that wins you the blackberry. The French word
for orange, which is *orange*. Monarchs eat
only milkweed, and are named for kings.
Sometimes the king is bad, or mad, a word
which can mean angry, or that something's off
in someone's mind. Your mother likes to see
you kiss your sister, and your mother scares
you sometimes, when you won't get into bed.
Pokeweed, tansy, Chinese lantern flower,
the poisonous profusion of the hill.
Pick it, don't touch it, this one, yes, no, yes.
The great book of injunctions: we can start
to pick out, word by word, instructions for
our lives, which, as we live, we learn to read.
That purple flower like a magic wand?
I'm sorry—no, I've never learned its name.

Collection

A few stones at a time
my son brings home the mountain.

How to Face Your Own Mortality and That of Your Loved Ones

I hit the panda button and pandas
are exploding out of the earth; abseiling
from trees like spiders over last night's
dinner beneath that ancient pine tree
on my grandparents' terrace. Some day, will I
be as tall as my father? What keeps eating
my parents? Look: a motley panda
in the swimming pool, spouting like a whale; a panda's parachute
slackening, opening again, like an enormous, beating,
black, white, black, white heart.

Parental Authority Is a Myth like Any Other Myth

Speaking of which, where are our robot sharks?
Two, four, six, eight, whom do we repudiate?
Animals! Why do you keep doing bad things?
You've been growling furiously all afternoon,

"Two, four, six, eight, whom do we repudiate?"
Asking the question doesn't change the answer
you've been growling furiously all afternoon.
Where and just how fast are you going?

Asking the question doesn't change the answer
unless you're addressing a photon.
Where and just how fast are you going
to build your new city? Utopia,

unless you're addressing a photon.
Animals! Why do you keep doing bad things
to build your new city, Utopia?
Speaking of which, where are our robot sharks?

Hands

All that ride home I
bit the inside of my lip to keep
from cursing, so as not to frighten
the children. I had closed the door
on one thumb

and as the nail
blued and swelled, I curled
about it the other hand's fingers,
warm around the shock and
fear. So you hold me.

IV. Third Body Paragraph

A Long List of Small Mercies

I.

But we have deferred by a year our son's first active shooter drill.

II.

Instead, he has A) learned 1) to make a) rice

b) pie crust

c) lego catapults

d) pop-up dinosaurs

e) a stuffed sloth with embroi-
dered eyes

f) the best of things

2) to add, but not to subtract

3) to identify a) red-tail hawks

b) doves

c) barn owls

d) rabbit tracks

e) raccoons

4) to read

5) only what he had to about death

B) drawn a thousand penciled 1) tyrannosaurs

2) dragons

3) sketches of our house
in spring

C) climbed fallen tree trunks

D) watched 1) Looney Toons

2) Junkyard Wars, on the couch, leaning on
his father's shoulder

III.

Together we have A) made 1) air-dry clay violets

2) marble traps

3) the air ring with a) laughter

b) outrage

B) grown 1) tomatoes

2) green beans

3) one small pumpkin

IV.

Here in the little rooms of our house we have made a A) kingdom
$\qquad$ B) homestead
$\qquad$ C) commune
$\qquad$ D) bardo

V.

And A) although once he fell on the stairs
$\quad$ B) bled from his forehead
$\quad$ C) we did not dare to bring him to the hospital

VI.

the scar is tiny, a little star, the kind A) that seems small across trillions
$\qquad$ of miles
$\qquad$ B) made of burning hydrogen, like
$\qquad$ our sun
$\qquad$ C) we have taught him to wish on

Slope

When I think of him, my father ascends
                    the trail ahead of us

easily looking forward
                    pine trees framing the White Mountains

as bannisters frame his face
                    he goes without a backward look

he leaves us behind, heading
                    toward Tuckerman Ravine

toward bed along the dark hall
                    to the rush of ice crystals, vertigo, swift
                    descent

this man used to
                    awake at dawn to reach untouched snow
                    three miles up

bring me to the mountains
                    laughing from the tops of crags

vertigo, swift descent; he rises
                    steady, buoyed, held up

in a mechanical chair
                    unreachably far

Carboniferous

> A new study . . . suggests that the evolution of a type of fungi
> known as white rot may have brought an end to a 60-million-
> year-long period of coal deposition known as the
> Carboniferous period.
>
> —NSF

Nothing, they would have thought, if they had thought,
can break us down: here we will lie, until the world is wrapped,
a static chrysalis in thread upon thread upon thread of unchanging
trunks—meters deep, until the soil, unreachable beneath our weight,
is so occluded by our incorruptible trunks that no more will sprout.
Nothing can stop us. We are living rock. We re-make the world
in our own image.—Then, the surprise, if they could feel
surprise: white rot, the slow bloom, spread, and then, thank God,
decay. And in the air—that changing air, so rich, now, with their exhalations—
the first thin glitter of kaleidoscopic wings, and beneath their trunks
the scutter of proliferating feet, as leaves and leaves accrued around the mounds
of dead trees sinking slowly—forever, they would have thought—into the earth.

The Alien Observer Gets Worried

He'd had some qualms already, but the concern
really hit him hard the day
one of the animals placed in its mouth
a pellet of red ochre, chewed, then looked up
and blew onto the interior wall of a cave
a thin red film. This so clearly
lacked utility that it could be a sign
only of intelligence, which manifests
as whim. That was the moment
when he began to expect
that one tribe of apes would set a pattern
by exterminating another. That we would learn
how to construct consequences so complex
as to be unforeseeable. Fire had been bad,
but harmless, give or take a few savannahs;
this, though, the red circle, was a metaphor,
standing in for the sun, for inventing
and unleashing unthinkable infernos,
for I Was Here. A few chews and a blast of air
and a cave becomes a castle. This is it,
he thought, this is the end of this world.

Hill Country

Though they seem a landscape made for gardens—not ambitious
    sweeping grasslands to be sod-broken, or
obdurate, glacier-scrubbed granite heights
    to be warily ceded to the patched,
gap-toothed mountainfolk—these rolling hills between cities
    hide small dangers. Rocks that rise out of the meadow
each spring to snap a plough's tooth; thorned
    blackberry vines, waiting to catch an ankle;
the glossy, attractive sheen of poison ivy; all are
    perils of a sort. Around them, the topsoil
is unenriched, tannic from centuries of oak leaves.
    So when we dig the beds, we go far down:
past dark loam into near-sand, excavating stones laid
    like eggs by recent boulders. These hills,
apparently apprentice mountains, are what's left
    of crags that once outstripped the Himalayas.
They teach us modesty. "Plant what you like," they murmur,
    "and please your woodchuck, who, if you exile him,
will be replaced by another in a day or two. We
    can be mollified, briefly, with a few bags
of cow manure, some measured lime; drop milk of magnesia
    into the holes you make, never deep enough,
for the tomatoes. We might even feed you. Sunset,
    moonrise; a few months, and harvest.
It is not what we are made for. We were not made for
    any convenience of yours. If, like others,
you burrow root cellars in our sides, we may notice,
    but the mice that join you will not be our envoys.
Find in our unconcern, our equilibrium, your comfort.
    Go ahead; you can make this your home."

How to Survive a Wildfire

1. Find a safe spot

Look for the bare, the unpromising. Against your palms the grit of cast pebbles, the crackle of mica. Find the untender crack of a line of slate. Be the missing piece in this hard puzzle.

2. Retreat from the fire by running to a safe spot

Do not contest gravity. The slope is stronger than you are; borrow its strength. The glimmer uphill is a fallen birch, not a patch of stone. Fear does not lend wings. Somewhere in that field below, is it? a wide upwelling of the earth's bones.

3. Hunker down

Be barren. Shuck your husk like still-sheathed corn lest the silk blaze. Condense, narrow, refine, within your two hands. This is the air you breathe: in, out, in, from the pine-needle richness. Before your eye a single leaf with three small lobes.

4. Consider burning out a spot to make your own safe zone

The scratch of a fingernail against rough sand. My hand in my pocket, searching for a remembered stone.

5. Run through the flames into the burned-out area

They tell you, you must face your fears. Place your hand in the box of snakes and you will never fear snakes again. You feel that dry slither, scale and scale against the raised hairs on your forearm, for hours as you wait your turn. Maybe there has been no error; perhaps nothing in that box has venom sacs intact. It is only your hand, only the left. Try it; what is the worst that could happen?

Call When You Get There

for CAM

The Milky Way, like crumbs on top
    of a vast galette—studded
with ripe planets, like figs—
    how you have enjoyed
everything you taste;
    as you pass Alpha Centauri,
please, find a radio signal
    sent to us by the sulphur beings
of the horsehead nebula,
    and into their code add instructions
for tasting this last bottle
    of the wine you left behind

The Migraine

The yeti sits in the best guest chair. I am a reasonable person, she thinks. If I stir six sugars into its cup, if I offer it milk, if I hand it the best chocolate for-company biscuits, perhaps it will behave. Perhaps when it leaves the only sign will be a few orange hairs on the chintz. It picks up the teacup, delicately, by the porcelain handle, cradles the saucer, sips. Yetis, perhaps, have an undeserved reputation. Perhaps if groomed with the cat's flea comb, if tenderly washed in rose-scented soap from the special soap shop, if given an ironed linen napkin on which to wipe its mobile turquoise lips, perhaps if I manage things reasonably, it will leave when a good guest should leave, when the sun's finished sinking and it's the hour to leaf through last week's magazines. Perhaps this time there will be no smash, no spin, no splintering, no furniture upended, no flailing dances; perhaps nothing at all will be twisted off my shoulders.

Dear Ilsabil,

                    You're right; in this seacoast hovel
there is nothing to love, not even your husband
or a picturesque thorny rosebush marring the whitewash;
blackbeetle, mice, leggy vermin with thick, crunchy shells
inhabit the thatch—one fell into your bed in the night last June
and when you rolled on it in your sleep it left subcutaneous stigmata.
You've given up on the soot blackening the rafters; it flakes off on your
   hand and disguises
the gray in your hair. No wonder you're outraged when your husband
   casts back
the talking fish, its magical offer unused, taking only his hook from its
shockingly human mouth. No wonder you call him a madman
and send him to scour the shoreline, demanding a cottage. Slate-roofed.
A firm wall between the kitchen grease and the white linen on your firm
   new mattress.
Don't stop there. Require a house, half-timbered. It should have a dining
   room, study, nursery
for any progeny this sweet new air and unfamiliar comfort may
engender. Aim higher—a palace: beauty, ease, a library, a stained-glass
   chapel
dedicated to your use. Send your husband out to find again that bleeding,
   cold, ironic-eyed
creature and tell it, "Ilsabil would be queen." Think
of the fleets of servants, scrubbing the flagstones for you, bringing you
seeds broken from a pomegranate, to scrape luxuriously between your
   teeth.
Think of placing your feet, in blue satin slippers, on a cushion. But
stop there. Don't ask for more. Don't send him again to say, "She wants
to be pope." You're right; of course you're right; you could do a better job
of ordering all this; those years of rolling up your fraying cotton sleeves
and plunging your hands into water all but hot enough to scald, then
   lacing it with lye,
have made you fit better in vestments than any bastard-siring Borgia.

But don't—don't—cui bono? Why would you lose the grapes,
the hothouse that grew them, in favor of anything? Of power? Just this once,
keep him here, or send him to be shaved by the castle barber, scrubbed clean
and tended by, thank God, someone else's hands.

Night Shift, Summer, 1994

1. Renée Explains Things to the New Girl

Love is not
        everything;
                my girls need
cough drops,
        rainbow unicorn
                trapper keepers
to smear with
        blue erasable
                pens;
for this the
        fifty cents
                extra of the night
shift hours;
        for this, despite
                the rules,
I take home
        the still hot
                apple pies
destined
        by law
                for the huge
white sack;
        love is not
                edible;
love is not
        the thing Kent
                thinks it is;
love does not
        hang against
                anyone's
thigh,
        bounce askew
                like this month's
ridge-flawed
        happy meal
                superball;

is not what

        I carried for

                eighteen

months in my

        sweat-soaked

                uniform pants,

their open waist

        held in place

                with a tightening

band;

        love is not why

                I am here;

if love

        were what

                made me

a mother, Kent

        who will

                show you what

he thinks he

        is not,

                would be mother

to music;

        Sarah, who steals

                from the drawers,

would be

        mother

                to her own

independence;

        love is

                nothing,

is the nothing

        unbought by

                thirty-eight hours

of the smell

        of hot grease

                on the heat lamps;

things are

        the problem,

                not love.

2. Kent the Night Manager Invites Renée into the Walk-In Freezer

Please: nothing

    can satisfy: not

        the bricks of pressed

beef with their

    ridges of

        pre-drawn char,

not the salt

    shaken in

        trained arcs

mimicking the

    glowing *m*

        above us

onto sunny

    potatoes;

        not the keen

of Kiss

    FM radio

        crying over plastic

red and gold

    seats

        in the front;

nothing can

    give to me

        a seat in the dark

booth

    at the station

        spinning the

black sweet

    disks

        instead

of these

    blackened

        slabs;

I am sure

    you detect

        in me

an absence,
       that for you
              presence
is a sign
       of my failure;
              surely you know
that I dream
       of music,
              made body
only by
       the motion
              of air
against
       membrane;
              tender
desire made
       resilient
              familiar
flesh;
       you must feel
              what is absent
as keenly
       as I do;
              I can't
stand
       to explain it;
              come in,
I have
       something
              to show you.

3. Karla, Working the Drive-Thru, Answers a Man in a Pickup Truck

No, I

        will not

                meet you;

forever between

        us will remain

                the empty frame

of this window;

        tonight no one

                but the moon

will wait

        in the lot;

                although for this

I know

        the managers

                place the girls here,

at the front,

        the men sweating

                over the grill,

equally positioned

        so you can see

                on entering

brighter smiles;

        only Renée,

                thirty, fat,

may pass

        the barrier;

                no; I will

if I must

        remember that

                I inhabit

a body

        seek in this

                August heat

the walk-in

        freezer, which

                can kill a man;

will watch

        not you

                but my breath

made present
          made body
                    by cold;
last year
          in the play
                    I played a witch,
wore on my
          thin face
                    a spirit-gummed
beard, told
          the truth
                    to a man
who heard
          me lying
                    in dry-ice smoke;
three days ago
          some man sat
                    where you sit
holding between
          his window
                    and my window
a pistol,
          demanding only
                    my attention;
even he
          could not
                    pierce
the interval;
          always between
                    us will be
this distance,
          nothing
                    will pass it
but breath;
          you may inhale
                    but nothing
that I can
          withhold
                    will reach you.

The Pyramid

1.

To say that I am obsessed is to overlook
the many things I do; admittedly, every action is to be duplicated
somewhere in the pyramid, but meanwhile, here
I am at the store, left hand on the cart, right
reaching for fresh ginger, only one small part of my mind
thinking past clutching it, placing it in the cart, paying, driving,
waiting for evening, chopping it into disks,   .
then to matchsticks, dropping it in the oil—one part
of my mind, near the part that keeps the heart beating,
considering whether it will be best reproduced
in clay or in stone.

2.

The pyramid
grows slowly.
First the sketches,
then the trucked in
bricks, then reclaimed
paving stones, then sacks
of cement, requiring shelter.
Near them, in the yard, half up-
ended by last week's windstorm,
a row of conspiring wheelbarrows,
buckets, a sub-pyramid of tawny sand.
But how to arrange them? The bricks
are to line the hallways, but where
should the traps fall, and when
should I install them? How
to attach the walls' facing,
and at what angle should
I cement the unbuilt
buttresses to the
soon to be sunk
foundations?

3.

There are setbacks. Today, six cats, suspicious-eyed, arrayed
like draperies on an Edwin Weeks elephant, glossy,
relaxed, sprawl in what, roofed and filled, will be
the Chamber of Music.
One, on rags in the corner, threatens kittens.
Around them, drifts of fur, cat piss
filling eternity with ammonia.

4.

On the ping-pong table I have spread
modeling clay, three-inch bricks
of peach, carmine, canary, sepia;
taking form, rows of
tiny cadavers, my servants
to be buried with me:
a baker, in an apron, whom I must
remember to equip with
an oven and shelves of bread;
a stooped woman pushing
a vacuum cleaner; three lovely girls
in three combinations of
hair, skin, bikini.
A bicycle in wire. Cars,
six of them, each the best
of its decade, from
the hobby shop; next to them,
one inch tall, gas cans marked
5 Litres.

But where are the supply chains?
When this bread is eaten, when the flour
is exhausted, how in the millennia
will I and my servants
find more? It weighs on me; I line
the basement walls with newsprint sketches, designs
for bas reliefs: wheat fields, a distant tractor,
a kitchen garden, and far
on the horizon, oil wells, a refinery. Will
the figures sketched at their base
be sufficient to the pipeline,
its outlet valve to be placed
in the northwest wall?

5.

The neighbors are
unworried. Once reassured
no guns are in the slowly rising bunker,
they end the conversation.
The Smiths, to the east,
build a fence; to the west, the Mills
look away.

6.

I am not preparing for the end of the world. I am preparing for the world to last.
These blueprints would be maps of the tectonic plates, if only they'd stop shifting.
The walls are to be three feet thick at the base, brick reinforced with rebar, faced

with   stone,   filled
with   steel   risers;
I   hope   it is
fit   for   quakes,
fire,   dogs,   children,
construction,   floods,   even

the inevitable amnesia of irresponsible unlikely descendants; chambers filled with

the   needs   of   life.
One   room   for   food,
fruit,   sweets,   bread,   meat;
One   of   drink,   wine,
beer,   gin,   water;   One
is   the   library,   lined
with   books   I   have
not   yet   read;   One

is inhabited, for company, the girls, a wise-faced woman, two broad grinning men;

One   has   drums,
a guitar,   piano,   sheet
music;   One   is
lined   with   scenes
of   the   living,
teeming,   unmissable   world;

Only the least sympathetic observer could mistake these distances for miniatures;
And in the middle, a space capsule, a yacht cabin, the goal of the maze, furnished,
filled, still unbuilt, entirely planned, my quarters, centered around the sarcophagus.

7.

I am observing origins. Cloth comes from thread
comes from cotton comes from earth
tilled in the distance by someone, in-
finitesimally silhouetted against
the rain-cloud-threatened sky.
This is a map of the world, schematic,
but perfectly to scale, and in the center, nothing
but You Are Here. To say this is obsession
is to mistake the horizon
for the edge of the world,
to find oblivion in the vanishing point.

V. Conclusion

Narrative of the Tribal Bard

All the stories I love most are meat.
Let me recount the van-struck yearling doe
athwart the berm—how our whole clan
assembled, drawn by rot as vultures are,
to the thin, disputed eastern border
of our domain; how shortly then there came
the eastern clan, who wanted both the doe
and to establish right of precedent
by driving us away. We gorged and cawed
and gave no ground; wing against wing
we shoved and shouldered. There was meat for all—
for them, for us—and so we held palaver:
will this be an occasion to unite,
for now, perhaps through autumn, our two clans?
Though crows can kill each other, can drive off
unwanted interlopers, can exile
chick-eaters, food-thieves, stinkers, the obnoxious,
we also form alliances, expand
our flocks, sometimes to millions, in the times
when congregation is expedient.
So, with this doe: we picked the bones and scattered
the intestines. As we ate, we spoke:
—my youngest son is looking for a mate.
—we have some daughters. We'll let them decide.
—last summer we lost many to an illness.
—we too. it makes these border wars a bore.
—a truce, then?—truce.—those three dead oaks
for meeting place?—yes, parliament can sit
in those snapped branches.
                              So it was my son
and their three unclaimed daughters preened their tails
and shrugged their black-sheened shoulders. That's what meat
can bring us to: to mating, twenty years
of twig-built nests. Though corn will do, or wheat.
We have tales of famines; years of plague;
of orphans starving draggled in their nests;
but those are not my stories. I perform
before the clan our stories of abundance.
We eat them, jostling, shoving, all as one.

Steeple

Sometimes a window
opens, the song
changes key, not tragedy
but merriment.
Sparrows flit
in, out, in again
through the dream-holes
on the steeple —
not arrow slits, but piercings
to let in light, let loose
the peal of bells.

The Second Baby Explains the Unthinkable

You feared that you would love my brother more.
But terribly, you would love
each new child as you love me, as you love
him, with proprioceptive
selfishness; you could grow
a new child each year like a tender
limb budding from your body. Love does not
spread thin; it is not time,
to be allotted, not food, to be shared
until the plate is empty. That dream
in which your house grows new rooms
to hold the books you have never written?
That is love; and like the dream
you cannot choose when it comes; you are a tangle
of ganglions and you will fire.
You are as boring as dawn:
we knew with precision that
the sun would rise at 6:44 AM
and that your child
would be to you another limb,
warm and capable of pleasure, strength, pain.
So the morning sky was clear; so my eyes
for the moment blue; these are
incidentals of light. You are only the next
of billions to feel in your body
the shock of your baby's first breath.
You can imagine
the dislocation of the shoulder,
your arm visibly out of true. Now think of your body
if I were taken. Think of me absent;
you take a drink of water, feel
ice against your lips. That shiver;
you would think,
no—is she cold?

Old Joke

An old man goes to his doctor and says,
Doctor, how long have I got?
    (This joke is to be told in a descending intonation,
    with echoes of the man behind the fish counter
    calling number ninety-two, and the whirr
    of the coffee grinders, and the tinny
    smell of refrigeration holding in check
    the thousands of dollars of imported cheese;
    this joke contains gold-wrapped three-pound bars of chocolate
    and apricot jam and rye bread, which can be sliced or left whole,
    or sold by half loaves if there's no one else at home;
    when it's done being told, this joke will be getting on the crosstown bus
    and riding with big plastic bags lined with paper
    through the park on 79th Street to the east side
    where the old women wear white sneakers
    beneath their long mink coats;
    this joke will walk four blocks north from the bus stop
    through the sliding glass doors, nodding to the doorman,
    up to the apartment it's lived in for twenty-seven years,
    alone for the last eight, where it will wrap
    cheese and halvah and chocolate and a flat
    of smoked salmon in yesterday's *Times*
    to overnight to a girl in college reading too seriously
    and not cleaning her room and from the look of her starving)
And the doctor says, well, I'm not saying you're going to die,
but don't buy any green bananas.

Packing List

—twenty-first birthday, aching-cold brilliant January, insides of my wrists scraped clean by your unshaven cheeks, that poor boy giving me Dostoevsky, thirty people in a tiny, gritty room—

—deck of the ferry, sunrise, August chill, islands whose trees were felled for ancient boats, the humps of dolphin backs as we near Piraeus—

—left-hand lion of an Assyrian portal, extending the lines too far in the name of perspective, in the preservationist cool of the Metropolitan—

—migratory flash of an oriole, certainty that this time, yes, there would be a baby—

—nubbed cotton hospital blankets, three-foot drifts of record-breaking snow—

—the same oriole, lantern in rhododendron leaves—

—on Lake Manyara, density of feathered bodies, white, rose, vermillion, almost in tears as I learn to say *nimefurahi sana*, I am very happy—

—the splay of newly liberated limbs, purple, greased with vernix, the cheep of a robin chick—

—dawn, from my scapulae, invisible wings—

—what else to pack for the journey?

Notes

"Variations on a Theme by Oscar Wilde": Oscar Wilde, "Phrases and Philosophies for the Use of the Young," in Miscellanies. Project Gutenberg, www.gutenberg.org/files/14062/14062-h/14062-h.htm.

"Dreams from the Eastern State Pen, 1829" imagines the experience of one of the first prisoners in the Eastern State Penitentiary in Philadelphia, Pennsylvania, which was run by reformers following Benthamite principles. Inmates in the prison were (at least initially, until the building became overcrowded) kept in prolonged solitary confinement and given Bibles; they also had regular access to the outdoors in tiny private exercise yards adjacent to their cells, and were encouraged to learn trades.

"Carboniferous": The epigraph is taken from "Study on Fungi Evolution Answers Questions about Ancient Coal Formation and May Help Advance Future Biofuels Production." National Science Foundation, June 28, 2012, www.nsf.gov/news/news_summ.jsp?cntn_id=124570#:~:text=A%20new %20study%2D%2Dwhich,known%20as%20the%20Carboniferous%20 period/.

"How to Survive a Wildfire": The section headings are taken from Emily Guerin's article "How To Survive: 5 Tips for Hikers Caught In A Wildfire." LAist, September 10, 2020, https://laist.com/news/climate-environment/the-big-burn/how-to-survive-a-wildfire-tips/.

Publication Acknowledgments

The following poems have appeared in the following publications, sometimes in slightly different forms:

"Dreams from the Eastern State Pen, 1829," *Atlanta Review*; "The Migraine," "Your Airplane," and "Entropy," *Connotation Press*; "Renée Explains Things to the New Girl," *Diagram*; "Call When You Get There," *Moist Poetry Journal*; "The Second Baby Explains the Unthinkable," *The Nation*; "Parental Authority Is a Myth like Any Other Myth," *Olney Magazine*; "Optics Lab," *Psaltery & Lyre*; "For a Child Drowned Off Lesbos," *Rise Up Review*; "Lost in the Woods," *Southern Poetry Anthology: Volume V, Georgia*; "The Alien Observer Gets Worried," *Sou'wester*; "Self-Portrait as Noble Pen Shell," "Collection," *Split Rock Review*; "Five-Paragraph Essay on the Body-Mind Problem," *Spoon River Poetry Review*; "Units of Measure," *Stone Circle Review*; "Syllabus," *SWWIM Every Day*; "Old Joke," Two Serious Ladies; "The Reef," *The Yale Review*. "The Pyramid" and "Night Shift, Summer, 1994" first appeared in *Antiphonal Fugue for Marx Brothers, Elephant, and Slide Trombone*, Finishing Line Press, 2015.

Personal Acknowledgments

This book exists because of the help and kindness of many people.

Tremendous thanks to Robert Pinsky and the lovely people at Wesleyan University Press, especially Suzanna Tamminen, Oliver Eggers, John Murillo, Katie Smith, and Jim Schley.

Thank you to the teachers who have read and commented on poems from this collection, particularly Terrance Hayes, Rachel Hadas, Kate Daniels, Jamaal May, Tomás Morín, and my fellow students in the workshops at Bread Loaf Writers' Conference.

Thank you to Framingham State University's Center for Excellence in Learning, Teaching, Scholarship, and Service for their support, and to my colleagues at FSU, particularly Lisa Eck, Sandy Hartwiger, Evelyn Perry, Patricia Horvath, Desmond McCarthy, Bart Brinkman, Colleen Coyne, Jenn DeLeon, Sam Witt, and Talia Adry. Thank you also to friends and colleagues at Agnes Scott College: Peggy Thompson, Christine Cozzens, Charlotte Artese, Nicole Stamant, Amy Lovell, and the Caloric Intake Seminar.

Love and gratitude to the witty, inspiring friends who somehow turned the plague year into a writing year: the brilliant Stephanie Burt and the glorious Harpies, Catherine Rockwood, Luba Ostashevsky, and Jenn Lewin.

Thank you to Dana Goldman, Becca Boggs, Michael Wenthe, Isaac Cates, Matthias Ferber, Rebecca Ferber, Margaret Litvin, Christy Palmer, and Dave Scott; Krista Trousdale, Michael Sullivan, Molly Sullivan, Ilona Trousdale, John Bemben, Ben Trousdale, Elka Malkis, John Trousdale, Christine Trousdale, Geoffrey Trousdale, and Erin Trousdale; Fay Beauchamp, Gary Beauchamp, Ray Beauchamp, Quiara Hudes, Cecilia Beauchamp, and Julian Beauchamp; Mary Rivet and Miranda Meyer (and, through the empyrean, to Chris and John Meyer).

Most of all, thank you to my parents, Bill Trousdale and Priscilla Meyer; my children, Rafi and Ellie Beauchamp; and my spouse, Nick Beauchamp. These poems are for you.

About the Author

Rachel Trousdale is a professor of English at Framingham State University. Her poems have appeared in *The Nation*, *The Yale Review*, and a chapbook, *Antiphonal Fugue for Marx Brothers, Elephant, and Slide Trombone*. She is also author of the books *Nabokov, Rushdie, and the Transnational Imagination* and *Humor, Empathy, and Community in Twentieth-Century American Poetry*. She lives in Massachusetts with her spouse and two children.